# THE GRILLING GUIDE FOR OUTDOOR GRIDDLES

Katherine & Nicolas Love

# DEDICATION

This book is dedicated to our loving and supportive parents, who have always taught us that we can succeed at anything we want to accomplish.

Gary & Paula Bordelon
Tim & Patsy Love


And always for James Otto

# CONTENTS

# 1

# GETTING STARTED ON YOUR OUTDOOR GRIDDLE

# Cleaning your outdoor griddle cooktop

Once you receive your outdoor griddle, and periodically throughout the life of the griddle, you will want to clean and season the griddle top for enhanced cooking. The more you use and cook on your outdoor griddle, the better seasoned your griddle top will become.

To Clean: Use dish soap and water to clean your griddle and remove any dust when you receive it. Rinse well. Your griddle is ready to go.

To season: Seasoning is a simple process. Just heat your griddle top, add some cooking oil and spread the oil carefully over the cooking surface. Allow the griddle to heat and absorb oil for a few minutes, then get cooking!

Remember, like a good cast iron skillet, the more you cook on your outdoor griddle, the better seasoned it will become.

# Using the best tools

You can find our accessories, must-have outdoor griddle tools and more at www.backyardhibachi.com or in retail stores where outdoor griddles are sold.

### Cooking Utensils
2 spatulas & a scraper

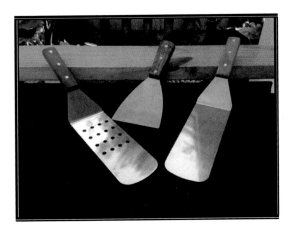

### Cheese Melting Cover
Useful for melting cheese on top of your creations, helping to speed cooking and also adding a little steam when needed.

### Carry All Caddy
This handy carrier holds all your oils, sauces and seasonings for easy organization on your griddle griddle .

# Cooking Tips

We encourage you to experiment! Use these recipes as a guide to get started and then create your own. Get started by substituting your favorite vegetables and meats into our recipes. Visit www.backyardhibachi.com or search YouTube for video instructions on griddle tricks, like the crowd-pleasing onion volcano. Any meal you could grill, sauté, fry, steam, sear or flambé; you can do it all on your outdoor griddle!

Reuse an old beer or soda six pack holder as a great carrier for your oils, squirt bottles and seasonings.

Plastic squeeze bottles are great for holding oils and fresh water to clean the griddle top with, as well as make it easy to squirt high proof alcohols like Bacardi 151, for your flambéed desserts.

The center of the griddle over the burner is going to be your main cooking area. The sides and corners of the griddle top are a great place to keep food warm while you are cooking another part of the meal.

Use your griddle scraper and water to "steam clean" your griddle top in between courses and scrape any debris into your removable drippings tray.

# The Best Oils

We always keep several different oils around the house for using in different recipes on the outdoor griddle. Many of the oils used in our recipes are suggestions, but you can substitute them for your favorites.

In the Asian cooking aisle at many grocery stores, you can find stir fry oils, which often have garlic and other flavors infused into the oil. These make great cooking oils and add extra flavor to already flavorful recipes.

Grapeseed oil is great high-heat cooking oil that has a light flavor that won't overpower your dish.

Coconut oil cooks well on the griddle at any heat and can add delicious, fresh flavor to any dish.

Avocado oil is another good high heat cooking oil.

Toasted sesame oil is great for cooking with and to add toasty flavor to any dish.

# 2
# APPETIZERS

Fabulous finger foods for your audience to enjoy while
you entertain with the next course!

# Ribeye Bites

2 Ribeye steaks (we like at least 1 and 1/2" Thick cut)

Seasonings to taste: Garlic Powder, Onion Powder, Salt, Pepper or mixed Cajun Seasoning

1 cup Italian Dressing

1/4 cup Worcestershire sauce

1 Jalapeno sliced and seeds removed.

Slice meat into cubes or strips as wide as the meat is thick. Season meat to personal preference and place in covered Tupperware or Ziploc bag with the remaining ingredients. Mix the contents and place inside refrigerator to marinate for at least 3-5 hours prior to cooking.

To cook: Preheat griddle to medium heat and pour meat onto outdoor griddle cooktop. Stir-fry until meat is cooked to desired temperature and sauce is caramelized on meat.

# Skewered Shrimp

2 pounds of fresh peeled shrimp

Italian Dressing

Seasonings to taste

Bamboo Skewers

Toss shrimp in ½ cup of Italian Dressing and your preferred seasonings.

Add 5-6 shrimp to each skewer, leaving at least 2 inches of bare space on the skewers for holding and flipping.

Heat griddle to medium heat and oil with your favorite high temperature cooking oil. (See Chapter 1 for suggestions)

Place skewers on griddle and cook for 3-4 minutes on each side, adjusting time for the size of your shrimp.

# Grilled Halloumi Cheese

2- 8 ounce packages of Halloumi Cheese

Olive Oil

Red Pepper Flakes

Onion Powder

Cut Halloumi cheese into strips about 1 in. by 3 in. Drizzle with olive oil and season with red pepper flakes, onion powder and salt.

Oil and preheat griddle to medium heat. Grill cheese for 2-3 minutes on each side or until warmed through. Serve immediately.

Halloumi cheese gets soft and chewy when grilled, instead of melting like most cheeses, so it is a perfect finger food. You can also opt to put it on bamboo skewers for easy grilling and eating.

Instead of red pepper flakes:

Try fresh or dried thyme instead for a different flavor

Or season with Herbs de Provence for a French flair.

# Bacon Wrapped Shrimp

2 pounds of large peeled shrimp

Block of jack cheese

3 fresh jalapenos

1 pack of bacon

Toothpicks

Seasoning

Clean and devein shrimp. Season raw shrimp with your favorite seasonings. Cut bacon strips in half. Cut jack cheese into squares, about 1 inch wide, ¼ inch thick. Cut jalapenos in half, take out seeds and then slice into strips. On each large shrimp, stack a square of cheese and a strip of jalapeno. Wrap in bacon and secure with toothpicks. Try to surround shrimp with bacon as much as possible, to prevent cheese from leaking out as it melts.

Oil griddle top on medium heat. Cook bacon wrapped shrimp for a few minutes on each side, or until bacon has reached desired crispiness. Enjoy!

# Bacon Wrapped Stuffed Jalapenos

6-8 fresh jalapenos

8 oz. pack of cream cheese

1 pack of bacon

Toothpicks

Cut Jalapenos in half and scoop out seeds. Fill cavity of peppers with softened cream cheese. You may want to cut bacon strips in half, depending on the size of your jalapeno peppers. Wrap thoroughly with bacon and secure with toothpicks. Try to cover the length of the pepper as much as possible to keep cream cheese inside.

Oil griddle top on medium heat. Cook bacon wrapped jalapenos for a few minutes on each side, or until bacon has reached desired crispiness. Enjoy!

# Grilled Caprese

2-3 ripe tomatoes, sliced into 1/4in. thick rounds

Shredded mozzarella cheese

Chopped fresh basil

Olive oil

Balsamic vinegar

Mix cheese and basil in a bowl and set next to griddle . Sprinkle tomato slices with salt and pepper.

Use olive oil to oil the griddle top on medium heat.  Sear tomato slices for 1 minute on one side.  Flip tomato slices and immediately top each slice with a pinch of basil-cheese mixture and allow to melt.

Once cheese begins to melt, drizzle with balsamic vinegar and serve.

# Lettuce Wraps

1 tablespoon olive oil

1 pound ground chicken

2 cloves garlic, minced

1 onion, diced

1/4 cup hoisin sauce

2 tablespoons soy sauce

1 tablespoon rice wine vinegar

1 tablespoons freshly grated ginger

1 teaspoon Sriracha, or more, to taste

1 (8-ounce) can whole water chestnuts, drained and diced

2 green onions, thinly sliced

Salt and black pepper, to taste

1 head butter lettuce

Heat olive oil on griddle top over medium high heat. Add ground chicken and cook until browned, about 5 minutes, making sure to crumble the chicken as it cooks; push cooked chicken to the side of the griddle.

Whisk together garlic, onion, hoisin sauce, soy sauce, rice wine vinegar, ginger and Sriracha in a bowl and then pour onto griddle and cook until onions have become translucent, about 1-2 minutes. Stir in water chestnuts and green onions until tender, about 1-2 minutes; season with salt and pepper, to taste. Mix together with chicken.

To serve, spoon several tablespoons of the chicken mixture into the center of a lettuce leaf, taco-style.

# 3
# Fried Rice

An outdoor griddle cooking staple.
Get creative with fried rice, the sky is the limit.
Learning egg tricks will keep you and your family
entertained for years.

# Shrimp Fried Rice

1pound of peeled shrimp
1 onion (chopped)
1 bag frozen mixed vegetables
2-3 cups rice (cooked)
1/4 cup soy sauce (to taste)
1/2 stick butter
1 tsp minced garlic
2 eggs

Generously oil griddle prior to cooking and re-oil between ingredients. High temperature cooking oil recommended. (See Chapter 1 for suggestions.)

Place cooked rice to one corner of griddle top. Put butter on top of rice pile and allow to melt.

Sauté onion and garlic on medium heat and cook until done. Add mixed vegetables and cook until hot. Move onion and vegetables to the side of the griddle top. Sauté shrimp until done, then move to side of griddle top.

Crack eggs and scramble. Chop up egg and mix in rice, cooked shrimp and veggie mix, add soy sauce and seasoning to taste and serve once heated and combined. Enjoy!

# Bacon Fried Rice

1/2 pack bacon, chopped
1 onion (chopped)
1 bag frozen mixed vegetables
2-3 cups rice (cooked)
1/4 cup soy sauce (to Taste)
1/2 stick butter
1 tsp minced garlic
2 eggs

Generously oil griddle prior to cooking and re-oil between ingredients.
High temperature cooking oil recommended.
(See Chapter 1 for oil suggestions.)

Place cooked rice to one corner of griddle top. Put butter on top of rice
pile and allow to melt.

Place bacon, onion and garlic on medium heat and cook until done.
Add mixed vegetables and cook until hot. Move bacon and vegetables to the
side of the griddle top.

Crack eggs and scramble. Chop up egg and mix in rice, cooked bacon
and veggie mix, add soy sauce to taste and serve once heated and combined.
Enjoy!

# Hawaiian Fried Rice

1 can of pineapple tidbits
1 cup chopped ham
1 onion (chopped)
1 tsp minced garlic
1 bag frozen peas
2-3 cups rice (cooked)
Soy sauce (to Taste)
1/2 stick butter
2 eggs

Generously oil griddle prior to cooking and re-oil between ingredients. High temperature cooking oil recommended. (See Chapter 1 for suggestions.)

Place cooked rice to one corner of griddle top. Put butter on top of rice pile and allow to melt.

Place onion and garlic on medium heat and cook until done. Add peas, ham and pineapple and cook until hot. Move to the side of the griddle top.

Crack eggs and scramble. Chop up egg and mix in rice, cooked ham and veggie mix, add soy sauce to taste and serve once heated and combined. Consider serving in a halved, hollowed out pineapple for a festive touch.

# Quinoa & Broccoli Fried "Rice"

2 cups of quinoa, cooked according to package
1 onion (chopped)
1 bunch of broccoli, broken into bite-sized pieces
1 tsp minced garlic
1 bag frozen peas & carrots
Soy sauce (to Taste)
1/2 stick butter
2 eggs

Generously oil griddle prior to cooking and re-oil between ingredients. High temperature cooking oil recommended. (See Chapter 1 for suggestions.)

Place cooked quinoa to one corner of griddle top. Put butter on top of quinoa pile and allow to melt.

Place broccoli, onion and garlic on medium heat and sauté until done. Add peas and carrots and cook until hot. Move to the side of the griddle top.

Crack eggs and scramble. Chop up egg and mix in quinoa, cooked broccoli and veggie mix, add soy sauce and seasoning to taste and serve once heated and combined.

Optional: Add your favorite meat or seafood to this recipe

# 4
# Lo Meins & Noodle Dishes

### Another outdoor griddle favorite!

Experiment with your favorite meats and veggie combos, Lo Mein is a great, versatile dish.

# Shrimp Lo Mein

1 pound of peeled shrimp
1 pack of spaghetti
1 diced onion
Pack of frozen mixed veggies
Soy sauce
Grapeseed oil
Toasted sesame oil
Minced garlic
Seasoning
Butter

Cook spaghetti according to package directions, set aside.

Oil griddle top and heat to medium heat. Sauté onions and minced garlic. Add mixed veggies once onions have started to become translucent and stir fry until all is cooked to tender-crisp. Push veggies to the side of the griddle top. Add 2 tbsp. of butter and shrimp to griddle top. Season shrimp with your favorite seasoning as you sauté until cooked through. Push shrimp to side.

Re-oil griddle if needed. Add pasta to griddle top. Mix in shrimp and cooked veggies. Dash with toasted sesame oil and soy sauce to taste. Stir fry Lo Mein, scraping and tossing, but allow to stick a little for that good sticky Lo Mein quality, if desired. Once noodles have reached desired doneness, enjoy!

# Chicken or Beef Lo Mein

1 pound of thin sliced chicken or beef
1 pack of spaghetti
1 diced onion
1 bunch of broccoli
Pack of sliced mushrooms
1 cup shredded carrots
Soy sauce
Grapeseed oil
Toasted sesame oil
Minced garlic
Seasoning
Butter

Cook spaghetti according to package directions, set aside.

Oil griddle top and heat to medium heat. Sauté onions, shredded carrots and minced garlic. Add mushrooms once onions have started to become translucent and stir fry until all is cooked to tender-crisp. Push veggies to the side of the griddle top. Sauté broccoli with toasted sesame oil until tender-crisp. Push aside.
Re-oil griddle . Cook chicken or beef until done. Re-oil griddle if needed. Add pasta to griddle top. Mix in meat and cooked veggies. Dash with toasted sesame oil and soy sauce to taste. Stir fry Lo Mein, scraping and tossing, but allow to stick a little for that good sticky Lo Mein quality, if desired. Once noodles have reached desired doneness, enjoy!

# Spaghetti Squash Lo Mein

## A great low carb alternative

1 medium spaghetti squash
1 cup shredded carrots
1 bag frozen peas
1 can sliced water chestnuts
2 Tbsp. minced garlic
1 chopped onion
Grapeseed oil
Soy sauce
Shrimp or other meat (optional)

Cut spaghetti squash in half and scoop out seeds. Place cut side down in a baking dish with ½ inch of water and bake in oven for 1 hour at 350 degrees. When done, flip over and allow to cool. (This can be done ahead of time) Shred squash inside with a fork and set aside.

Oil griddle top and heat to medium heat. Sauté onions, shredded carrots and minced garlic. Add peas and water chestnuts once onions have started to become translucent and stir fry until all is cooked to tender-crisp. Push veggies to the side of the griddle top. Re-oil griddle . Cook shrimp until done.

Add shredded spaghetti squash and mix with veggies. Add soy sauce and toasted sesame oil to taste, along with seasoning if desired. Sauté until all is heated through, allowing to stick and scraping bottom, if desired.

# 5
# Vegetables &
# Side Dishes

Don't stop with the meat; create your entire meal on
your outdoor griddle! As many courses as you like!

# Awesome Asparagus

1 bunch of fresh asparagus
Butter
Salt
Pepper

Trim ends of asparagus off and wash.  Melt 2-3 tablespoons of butter on your griddle at medium heat. Stir fry asparagus in butter, adding salt and pepper to taste, until tender.

# Zucchini Squash Medley

2 zucchini
2 yellow longneck squash
1 bunch of broccoli
1 cup of shredded carrots
Soy sauce
Toasted sesame oil

Slice zucchini and yellow squash and chop broccoli into small florets. Oil griddle and sauté broccoli and carrots until starting to brown. Add squash and zucchini and continue to sauté until everything is tender-crisp. While cooking, add soy sauce and toasted sesame oil for flavor.

# Sesame Broccoli

1 bunch of broccoli
Toasted sesame oil
Sesame seeds
1 orange or red bell pepper
Soy sauce

Break broccoli into small florets.  Slice bell pepper and remove seeds. Oil griddle top with toasted sesame oil on medium heat. Sauté broccoli and bell pepper until tender crisp.  Add soy sauce or other seasoning to taste. Top with sesame seeds before serving.

# Sautéed Spinach & Mushrooms

1 pound of fresh spinach
1 pack of sliced baby bella mushrooms
Salt
Pepper
Grapeseed oil (or your favorite cooking oil)
Feta cheese

Oil the griddle top with grapeseed oil on medium heat. Sauté sliced mushrooms until done. Add spinach, season with salt and pepper to taste and sauté until wilted. Serve and sprinkle feta cheese on top.

# Loaded Smashed Potatoes

A perfect complement to your steak dinner, a version of the loaded baked potato for your outdoor griddle!

1 pound of small potatoes (small Yukon golds or a sunshine mix works well)
Grapeseed oil
Grated cheddar cheese
½ pack bacon, chopped
Green onions, chopped

Boil potatoes until tender, about 20 minutes. This can be done ahead of time. Cook chopped bacon until desired crispness is reached and move to side of the cooktop. Add grapeseed oil to bacon grease on cooktop, if needed. Put potatoes onto cooktop and gently smash them with a meat hammer. Drizzle tops with grapeseed oil and once the bottoms have started to brown, flip the potatoes. Top with cheddar cheese, bacon and green onions and serve once the other side of the potato has become nice and browned.

# Szechuan Eggplant

2 medium eggplant, peeled and cubed into 1 inch pieces
Salt and pepper
Green onions
Cornstarch
1-2 Tbsp. Szechuan Chili Paste
1 tsp soy sauce
1 tsp black Chinese vinegar
2 Tbsp. grapeseed oil
2 cloves garlic
1Tbsp of ginger root

Peel and chop eggplant into 1 inch chunks. Salt and set in colander over your sink to drain for 20-30 minutes. Once drained, lightly rinse and spread out on a paper towel on counter top to dry.

Dice green onions and add to eggplant. Place eggplant and onions back into colander and toss with just enough cornstarch to lightly coat. No more than a couple tablespoons or dish will be soggy. Mince the garlic and ginger root. Lightly sprinkle with pepper to taste.

Heat griddle top to medium high and add grapeseed oil, then add eggplant, garlic and ginger. Let eggplant brown on one side before tossing. Cook until the cubes are caramelized all over- about 4-5 minutes.

Turn down heat to medium low. Add 1-2 Tbsp. Szechuan Chili Paste, soy sauce, and Chinese vinegar. (If you enjoy more sauce you can add 1/4 cup of vegetable or chicken broth now or skip this for a drier, crispier dish.)

# Grilled Sweet Potato Fries

6 sweet potatoes, peeled
Grapeseed oil
Salt and pepper to taste


Boil the sweet potatoes until they are just barely cooked through. Drain and cool. This pre-boiling step can be optional, but it is the best way to have fully cooked and evenly browned fries.  Once cool, cut the potatoes into wedges or fries, then toss with a light amount of grapeseed oil. Oil and heat griddle top to high. Add sweet potato wedges and grill to crisp the outside, flip and then season to taste.

Optional seasonings: Cayenne and onion powder for spicy or cinnamon and sugar for sweet!

# 6
# Meat and Seafood

The Main Event.

# Sesame Chicken

3-4 boneless chicken breasts
Toasted sesame seeds
Grapeseed oil

Marinade:
6 tablespoons soy sauce
2 teaspoons toasted sesame oil
1 teaspoon kosher salt
4 tablespoons cornstarch
4 tablespoons water

For the Sauce:
3 tablespoons toasted sesame oil
1 teaspoon ginger, minced
1 clove garlic, minced
1 teaspoon chili paste
2 cups chicken broth
1/4 cup cornstarch
2 tablespoons rice vinegar
1/2 cup honey
2 tablespoons soy sauce

Cut chicken into 1 inch cubes. In a bowl, whisk marinade ingredients: soy sauce, toasted sesame oil, salt, cornstarch and water. Marinate chicken while making sauce. For sauce, whisk together all ingredients until combined.

Heat griddle to medium high. Oil with grapeseed oil and stir fry chicken until cooked through. Push aside. Pour sauce onto griddle top and let cook, stirring frequently until it begins to thicken. Mix chicken into sauce and toss to combine. Top with toasted sesame seeds. Serve over rice, if desired, with a side of 'Sesame Broccoli.'

# Teriyaki Chicken

1 pound of boneless chicken (breast or thighs)
1 diced onion
1 diced red bell pepper
1 bottle of Teriyaki sauce
(We like Kikkoman Original Teriyaki)
Grapeseed oil
Salt and pepper

Chop boneless chicken into 1 inch pieces. Season lightly with salt and pepper.  Heat griddle top to medium heat and oil with grapeseed oil.  Sauté diced onion and red bell pepper until done and push aside. Re-oil griddle top and sauté chicken pieces until cooked through. Mix in onions and bell peppers. Drizzle your favorite teriyaki sauce over chicken and toss to combine.  Cook until sauce is hot and evenly spread, allowing sauce to caramelize slightly. Serve immediately.

Excellent served over rice with our "Zucchini Squash Medley",
or as a stand alone dish

# Soft Shell Crabs

4 fresh soft shell crabs
Butter
Salt and creole seasoning
Flour (if desired)

Prepare soft shell crabs for cooking.  Look online for instructions. There are many videos showing how to prep and clean crabs.

Heat griddle to medium low. Lightly salt and season crabs. If desired, lightly dredge in flour. They are great without flouring though! Melt 2-3 Tbsp. of butter on griddle and put crabs on. Cook for 4-5 minutes on each side, or until done. Enjoy!

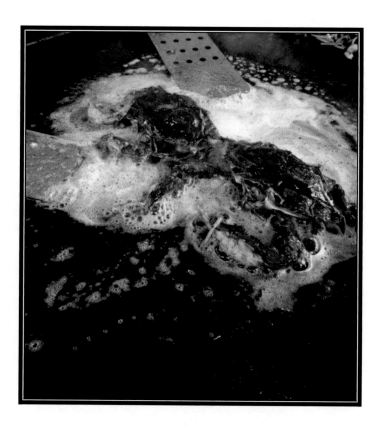

# Super Stir~Fry

1 pound of boneless chicken (breasts or thighs)
1 bunch of broccoli
1 can of baby corn
1 can of sliced water chestnuts
1 pack of sliced mushrooms
Soy sauce
Toasted sesame oil
Salt and pepper

Cut chicken into 1 inch pieces and season with salt and pepper. Chop broccoli into small florets. Oil griddle top and sauté broccoli and mushrooms until tender-crisp. While cooking, add soy sauce and toasted sesame oil for flavor. Push to side. Sauté chicken until done. Add baby corn, water chestnuts and cooked broccoli and mushrooms and toss to combine, adding soy sauce and a dash of toasted sesame oil, to taste.

Once combined and heated through, serve over white or brown rice, or with your favorite fried rice recipe.

# Sausage & Peppers

1 pound of Italian sausage
1 bell pepper
2 jalapenos (optional)
1 onion
Oil

Slice bell pepper and jalapenos into strips and take out seeds. Slice onion into strips. Heat griddle to medium high and oil. Cook sausage until cooked through, flipping as needing. Cut sausage into slices and push aside. Sauté onions, bell pepper and jalapenos until done.
Mix sausage in and cook until all heated.
Serve over rice, or as is.

Chef Favorite!

# Herbed Salmon

Filet of salmon
Herbs de Provence
Salt and pepper
Butter
Oil

Season your salmon with salt and pepper to taste and then sprinkle with Herbs de Provence (or you favorite seasoning). Oil griddle and heat to medium.

Griddle salmon, skin side down until top begins to split and fat turns white and bubbles out. This recipe may cook faster if salmon is covered with a BYH steamer cover for part of the cook time, but this is not necessary. When salmon is almost done, dot top with a little butter for extra flavor (optional).

Pairs nicely with our recipe for "Best Asparagus"

# Seared Sea bass

2 (4inch) pieces of Sea bass
4 Tbsp. of butter
Salt and pepper
Fresh Thyme or Parsley (optional)

Season Sea bass with salt and pepper.  Add fresh chopped thyme or parsley if desired.  Heat griddle top to medium and melt butter. Sear sea bass until golden brown on all sides.

This dish is great topped with sautéed mushrooms.

This recipe can also be used for delicious Seared Scallops or Shrimp.

# 7
# Cajun Favorites

Traditional Cajun recipes modified for your outdoor griddle! A little local flavor from the backyard of the original Backyard Hibachi.

Laissez les Bon Temps Rouler!

# Crawfish Étouffée Fried Rice

(Pronounced: ay-TOO-fay)

1 pack of peeled Louisiana crawfish
¼ cup oil for roux
½ cup flour
1 cup chopped onions
½ cup chopped bell pepper
½ cup chopped celery
Oil to sauté onions
Cajun seasoning
2-3 cups cooked white rice
½ cup of chicken broth

Heat griddle to medium and oil. Sauté onions, bell pepper and celery until onions are translucent. Add crawfish and sauté 3-4 minutes or until cooked, adding Cajun seasoning to taste as you stir. Push aside.

Heat griddle to medium and add oil for roux. Stir in flour, you want to create a thick paste for your roux. Brown flour, stirring often until you achieve a light coffee color. Add chicken broth and stir until roux is thoroughly mixed. Add in crawfish mixture and white rice. Toss until combined. Enjoy!

# Chicken & Sausage Sauce Piquante

(pronounced sos pee-kont)

4 boneless chicken breasts
1 pack of Cajun smoked sausage
Oil to sauté onions
¼ cup oil for roux
½ cup flour
1 cup chopped onions
½ cup chopped bell pepper
½ cup chopped celery
2-3 Tbsp. tomato paste
½-1 cup of chicken broth

Season chicken breasts and chop into 1 inch pieces. Slice sausage into ½ inch rounds. Heat griddle to medium and add oil. Sauté onions, bell peppers and celery until done and push aside. Re oil if necessary and sauté chicken, until cooked through. Add sausage and cook a few more minutes until all is heated. Push aside.

Heat griddle to medium and add oil. Stir in flour, you want to create a thick paste for your roux. Brown the flour, stirring often until you achieve a light coffee color. Add tomato paste and chicken broth and stir to combine. Let sauce cook for a couple of minutes, stirring as needed. Add more or less chicken broth if sauce is too thick or runny. Mix in chicken, sausage and onion mix until all is heated and well combined. Serve over rice.

# Shrimp & Grits

1 pound large peeled gulf shrimp
Cajun seasoning
1 chopped onion
2 cups of cooked, salted grits
Shredded cheese
Butter
Chopped green onions

Heat griddle to medium and oil.  Drop spoonfuls of grits on cooktop to make patties.  When grits patties start to brown, flip and brown other side.  Set aside. Re-oil griddle and sauté onions until translucent. Add 3 tbsp. of butter to melt and sauté shrimp until cooked through.

To serve, put several shrimp on top of each grit patty, top with some of the shrimp-butter sauce on the griddle and sprinkle shredded cheese and green onions on top. Yum!

# Cajun Ribeyes

2-3 ribeye steaks (we like 1 ¼ in thick)
1 cup of Italian dressing
¼ cup Worcestershire sauce
2-3 tbsp. Cajun seasoning (we like The Best Stop Cajun seasoning, but any good spicy mix will do)

Marinate your steaks at least 6 hours or up to 2 days ahead of time. The longer they marinate, the better they will be.  Put steaks in a large plastic container with a lid or large zipper lock bag. Add Italian dressing, Worcestershire sauce and Cajun seasoning. Mix together and let sit in refrigerator.

Heat griddle to medium high.  Sear steaks on both sides to your desired level of doneness. Optional: Carefully, use your long handled lighter and high proof alcohol when steaks are almost done, if you like that good, flame-broiled taste.

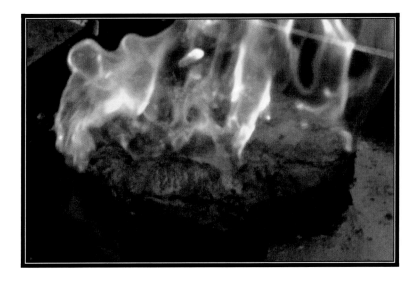

# Mardi Gras Veggie Medley

1 bunch of broccoli
1 bunch of purple cauliflower (if seasonally available)
1 yellow bell pepper
Grapeseed oil
Soy sauce
Toasted sesame oil

Cut broccoli and cauliflower into small florets. Scoop seeds out of bell pepper and slice into strips. Heat griddle to medium and oil with grapeseed oil. Sauté broccoli, cauliflower and bell pepper, until tender crisp. Add soy sauce and a dash of toasted sesame oil to taste as your veggies cook.

Enjoy this festive dish as a side at your Mardi Gras celebration, or anytime.

# 8
# Griddle Twists
# on Classics

Classic recipes made on your Outdoor griddle.
Everything tastes better outside!

# Hamburgers

1 pound ground hamburger
Your favorite seasonings
Sliced cheddar cheese

Season ground hamburger and form patties.  Heat griddle to medium and oil. Griddle hamburger patties, flipping as needed until desired doneness is reached.

Optional: We like bacon burgers, so we cook our bacon first (see bacon recipe on pg. 60 ) then cook burgers in the bacon grease, instead of oil. Yummy!

Top burgers with cheddar cheese and allow to melt. You can use your cheese melting cover for faster melting if you like.

# Steaks

Your favorite cut of steaks
Your favorite steak seasonings

Heat griddle to medium high. Sear steaks on both sides to your desired level of doneness. Optional: Carefully, use your long handled lighter and high proof alcohol when steaks are almost done, if you like that good, flame-broiled taste.

# Chicken, Steak or Shrimp Fajitas

Pick which meat, or use all 3

2-4 chicken breasts
1 flank steak
1 pound peeled shrimp
Olive oil
Chili powder
Ground Cumin
Garlic powder
Salt
Flour tortillas
Sour Cream
Shredded cheese
Sliced onion
Sliced bell pepper

Season your choice of meat liberally with olive oil, chili powder, cumin, garlic and salt. Let marinate for 4-6 hours.

Heat griddle to medium and oil surface. Sauté bell peppers and onions until done. Push to side. Cook your choice of meat until done. Slice chicken or beef into strips and serve on tortillas with shredded cheese and sour cream.

# Mushroom Jack Fajitas

2-4 Chicken breasts
Shredded Monterey jack cheese
8oz Sliced mushrooms
Flour tortillas
Sliced onion
Sliced bell pepper
4-5 slices of bacon
Sour cream
Diced tomatoes or pico de gallo

Season chicken breasts with salt and pepper. If desired, chicken can be marinated ahead of time. Heat griddle top and oil. Cook chicken breasts on both sides until done. Slice into strips and set to side of griddle top.

Sauté onions, bell pepper and mushrooms until starting to caramelize. Set aside.

Cook bacon until slightly crispy and coarsely chop.

Top each sliced chicken breast with mushrooms and onions, add a handful of shredded cheese and sprinkle with bacon. Allow cheese to melt.

Create fajitas by putting all this melty goodness in a tortilla and topping with sour cream and diced tomatoes or pico.

# Chicken Quesadillas

2-4 Chicken breasts
Shredded Monterey jack cheese
Flour tortillas
Sliced onions
Sour cream

Season chicken breasts with salt and pepper. If desired, chicken can be marinated ahead of time. Heat griddle top and oil. Cook chicken breasts on both sides until done. Slice into strips and set aside.

Sauté onions until starting to caramelize. Set aside.

Turn griddle heat to low. Put one tortilla on griddle top; add several slices of chicken, a few sautéed onions and a handful of cheese. Top with another tortilla. Flip when bottom tortilla is getting golden and cheese has begun to melt. When other side gets golden, transfer to plate and cut into triangles. Serve with sour cream and/or guacamole. Repeat with the rest of your ingredients.

# Grilled Chicken Caesar Salad

2 heads of romaine lettuce hearts
Fresh grated parmesan
Your favorite Caesar dressing
2 chicken breasts
Salt and pepper
Olive oil
Fresh baguette slices (optional)

Season chicken breasts with salt and pepper. If desired, chicken can be marinated in Caesar dressing ahead of time. Heat griddle top and oil. Cook chicken breasts on both sides until done. Slice into strips and set aside.

To make the crostini, (if desired) toast the baguette slices in a touch of oil directly on the griddle top until golden, set aside. Top with a sprinkle of parmesan, to melt.

Prepare the romaine lettuce by cutting the heart in half and drizzling with oil, then season with salt and pepper. On medium heat, griddle the romaine halves for approximately 1-2 minutes.

Transfer to plate, top with chicken slices and garnish with crostini and grated parmesan cheese. Drizzle the Caesar dressing over the assembled salad and enjoy!

# 9
# Desserts

Any outdoor griddle chef's grand finale. Test your
skills with these flambéed favorites!

# Bananas Foster

3-4 ripe bananas
3/4 cup brown sugar
1 tsp. cinnamon
Pinch of salt
4 tbsp. butter
Vanilla ice cream
¼ cup banana liquor
¼ cup high proof rum (Bacardi 151 or similar works well)
Long handled lighter (if flambéing; will be tasty without, also)

Cut bananas in half, and then in half again, lengthwise. Heat griddle to medium and melt butter. Add brown sugar and cinnamon and stir until completely dissolved, about 2 minutes. Add bananas and cook until they start to brown, about 3 minutes. Add banana liqueur and mix until just combined with bananas and caramel sauce.

Turn off griddle burner! Pour high proof rum (handy time to use a squeeze bottle, see Cooking Tips, in chapter 1) Carefully use your long handled lighter to ignite the rum. These steps must be done quickly together before the heat evaporates the alcohol. Let flame for 15-20 seconds to caramelize, then stir to put out flame if it hasn't already burned out.

Serve bananas and sauce on top of vanilla ice cream. Yum!

Tip: Measure out all ingredients ahead of time as this recipe cooks quickly.

# Cherries Jubilee

8 ounces of frozen black cherries
½ cup sugar
1 tbsp. cornstarch
1 lemon
3 tbsp. of butter
Vanilla ice cream
1/3 cup high proof rum (Bacardi 151 or similar works well)
Long handled lighter (if flambéing; will be tasty without, also)

Put cherries in a bowl to defrost. Squeeze ½ a lemon over them. Reserve juice in bowl. Mix sugar and cornstarch and set aside. Zest ½ the lemon. Strain defrosted cherries from their juice and save. Mix sugar and cornstarch with juice. Pour juice mix onto heated griddle griddle with 3 tbsp. of butter. Add cherries and lemon zest and cook until sugar is dissolved and cherries are cooked, about 4 minutes.

Turn off griddle burner! Pour high proof rum (handy time to use a squeeze bottle, see Cooking Tips, in chapter 1) Carefully use your long handled lighter to ignite the rum. These steps must be done quickly together before the heat evaporates the alcohol. Let flame for 15-20 seconds to caramelize, then stir to put out flame if it hasn't already burned out.

Serve cherries and sauce over scoops of vanilla ice cream.

# Caramelized Peaches & Ice Cream

3-4 ripe peaches
¼ cup honey
4 Tbsp. butter
1 tsp. ground ginger
Vanilla ice cream
¼ cup high proof rum (Bacardi 151 or similar works well)
Long handled lighter (if flambéing; will be tasty without, also)

Wash and dry, then slice peaches into wedges. Heat griddle to low- medium and melt butter.  Add honey and ground ginger and combine. Once combined and bubbling, add peaches and cook until tender and starting to brown.

If desired, flambé to caramelize:
Turn off griddle burner! Pour high proof rum (handy time to use a squeeze bottle, see Cooking Tips, in chapter 1) Carefully use your long handled lighter to ignite the rum. These steps must be done quickly together before the heat evaporates the alcohol. Let flame for 15-20 seconds to caramelize, then stir to put out flame if it hasn't already burned out.

Serve peaches and sauce on top of vanilla ice cream. Yum!

# 10
# Brunch

Don't forget the most important meal of the day!
Enjoy your coffee (or mimosas) in the fresh air as you
create brunch favorites on your outdoor griddle.

# Pancakes

Pancakes are a great option to feed a crowd for brunch.

Start with your favorite pancake recipe, or get those easy, just-add-water pancake mixes and heat the griddle.

Oil or butter the griddle top on medium heat and pour out your pancake batter into 3-4 inch rounds. Once batter bubbles on top and bubbles start to pop, flip for golden brown pancakes. Let other side cook until browned and start stacking them up on the side of the griddle . Enjoy with syrup and butter or fresh chopped fruit.

# Hash browns

2-3 large white potatoes
1 onion
1 bell pepper
Salt and pepper
Butter

Peel potatoes. Use cheese grater to shred potatoes. Chop onion and bell pepper into small chunks. Melt butter on griddle top, heat to medium. Sauté potatoes, onion and bell pepper, seasoning with salt and pepper as they cook. Cook and stir until potatoes are softened and starting to brown.

Serve with eggs and bacon, or top with cheese.

# Sweet Potato Hash browns

1-2 large sweet potatoes
1 tsp cinnamon
1-2 egg whites
Coconut oil

Peel sweet potatoes and shred with cheese grater. Mix sweet potato shreds with egg whites and cinnamon. You want the potatoes coated in egg white, but not wet. Heat griddle to medium and oil with coconut oil. Drop spoonfuls of potatoes onto griddle and flatten to make patties. Let cook for about 4 minutes and then flip and cook other side for
4 more minutes. Enjoy!

# Best Bacon Ever

Thick cut bacon is best.

Heat griddle to medium. Lay bacon slices on griddle . Flip when slices start to brown. Griddle to desired doneness.

Fry some eggs in the grease, if you like.

Warning: you may never want to cook bacon in your kitchen again! Your house won't smell like bacon for the next 3 days and no grease splatter on your clean stove top!

Added bonus: the griddle cooks the best chewy and crisp bacon we have ever made!

# French Toast

1 French baguette
4 eggs
½ cup milk
1 tsp. cinnamon
¼ tsp. nutmeg
2 tbsp. sugar
4 tbsp. butter
Maple syrup

Slice French baguette into 1 inch thick slices. Whisk together eggs, milk, cinnamon, nutmeg and sugar.

Heat griddle to med-low heat. Melt butter.  Dip bread slices in egg mixture and place on buttered griddle . When bottom starts to brown, flip bread and brown other side.

Enjoy with a drizzle of maple syrup and our "Best Bacon Ever"

# 11

# Outdoor Griddle Cooking Hacks

Simple Life Hacks and tips to help you get the most use out of your outdoor griddle.

While cooking, food can be set in corners of the griddle top to start warming or stay hot until serving.

Prep and chop ingredients ahead of time. Use ramekins or small bowls to measure out liquids and seasonings before cooking.

Use zipper locking bags to hold food and marinades together and dump directly on the griddle for easy cleanup.

An old beer or soda six pack holder makes a great carrier for your oils, squirt bottles and seasonings.

Plastic squeeze bottles are great for holding oils and fresh water to clean your griddle top with, as well as make it easy to squirt high proof alcohols like Bacardi 151, for your flambéed desserts.

## ABOUT THE AUTHORS

Katherine and Nic Love spend much of their time outside cooking for family and friends. Their collection of recipes is perfect for any cooking griddle or flat cooking surface you use in your backyard.

The Love family owns and operates Backyard Hibachi, LLC in Lafayette, Louisiana and loves spending time outdoors, creating new recipes and tricks on their own grills for family and friends to enjoy and are proud to be bringing other families together by sharing their recipes with others.

Made in the USA
Middletown, DE
17 July 2019